The Inventors' Club Meets Again

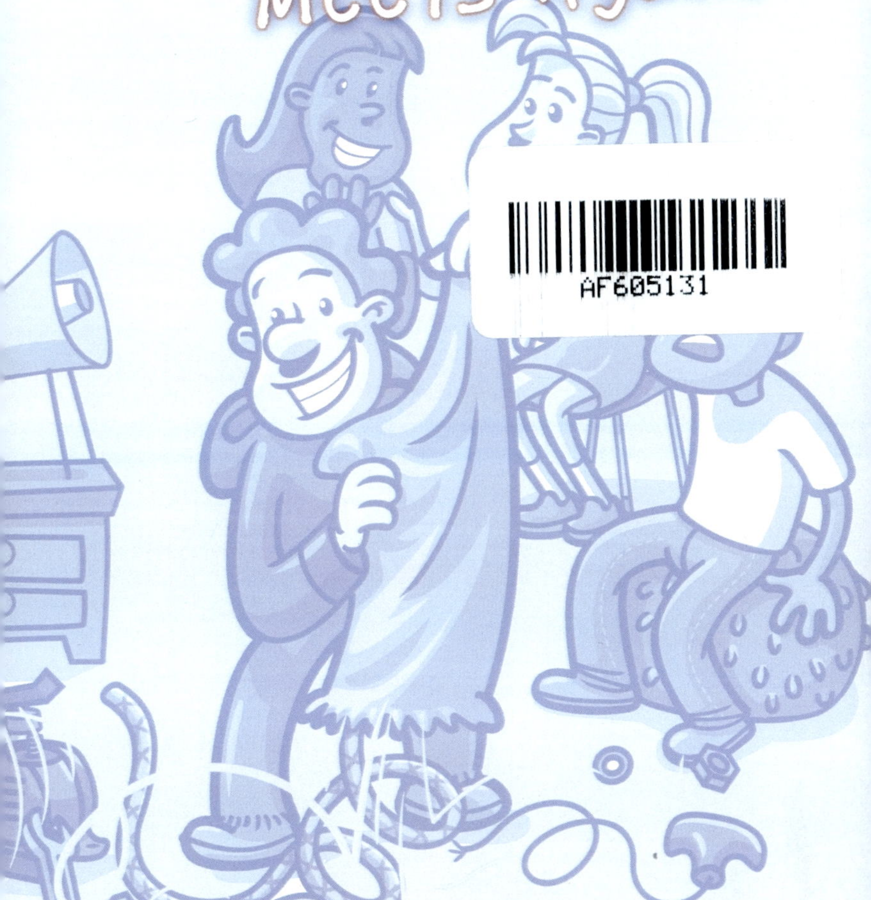

Nicolas Brasch
Phillip Small

Australia • Brazil • Japan • Korea • Mexico • Singapore • Spain • United Kingdom • United States

The Inventors' Club Meets Again

Fast Forward
Turquoise Level 18

Text: Nicolas Brasch
Illustrations: Phillip Small
Editor: Johanna Rohan
Design: James Lowe
Series design: James Lowe
Production controller: Seona Galbally
Audio recordings: Juliet Hill, Picture Start
Spoken by: Matthew King and Abbe Holmes

ISBN 978 0 17 012637 3
ISBN 978 0 17 012633 5 (set)

Cengage Learning Australia
Level 7, 80 Dorcas Street
South Melbourne, Victoria Australia 3205
Phone: 1300 790 853

Cengage Learning New Zealand
Unit 4B Rosedale Office Park
331 Rosedale Road, Albany, North Shore NZ 0632
Phone: 0800 449 725

For learning solutions, visit **cengage.com.au**

Printed in Australia by Ligare Pty Ltd
9 10 11 12 13 14 15 19 18 17 16 15

Evaluated in independent research by staff from the Department of Language, Literacy and Arts Education at the University of Melbourne.

The Inventors' Club Meets Again

Nicolas Brasch
Phillip Small

Contents

The Idea!

Ben, Chad, Bianca and Jodie held their Inventors' Club meeting on the third Thursday of every month. They took turns to show their new inventions.

Tomorrow was Ben's turn to show his new invention. The only problem was he hadn't thought of an invention yet ...

Ben was sitting at the kitchen table, eating a bowl of ice-cream.

"What can I make?" he asked himself as he ate his ice-cream.

Ben had no idea what he would invent.
He finished his ice-cream and went to get some more.
But, there was no ice-cream left.

"I know," he said, excitedly.
"I'll invent an ice-cream maker!"

Running Around

Ben grabbed some paper and a pen.
Then, he sketched a design
for his ice-cream maker.
The sketch didn't look much like
an ice-cream maker,
but Ben was sure it would work.

“I don’t need to test it,”
he said to himself.
"Well, I’m not going to have time
to test it.”

Ben only had time to get
the materials.

The next afternoon, Chad, Bianca and Jodie were in Chad's bedroom. Ben had turned up with a sack. He tipped the sack upside down, and many strange objects fell out.

"A pile of junk!" said Bianca. "That's a good invention."

"Ha, ha," said Ben. "Just wait and see."

The Ice-Cream Maker

The first object that Ben picked up was big, round and made of steel. It was the middle part of a washing machine.

Ben held up the part and looked through a hole in the bottom.

"Did you drill that hole?" asked Chad.

"Yes," said Ben.

"You didn't do a very good job," Chad said.

"As long as it works," Ben told Chad.

"Things have to look good as well, you know," said Chad.

Next, Ben grabbed a piece of hose and fitted it over the hole he had drilled.

"I think I know what it is," Jodie said, excitedly. "It's a mouse kennel!"

"A what?" asked Bianca and Chad together.

"A mouse kennel," said Jodie. "The mouse crawls through the hose and into its home."

Jodie often said strange things, but the others thought that this was one of the strangest things she had ever said.

Ben put a plastic ice-cream container on the floor and put the other end of the hose in it.
Then, he picked up a thin cord and wound it around the outside of the washing machine part.

When the cord had been wound tightly around the part, Ben stood back and looked at his invention.

"Well, what is it?" asked Bianca, Chad and Jodie together.

"It's an ice-cream maker, of course!" Ben said.

"How does it work?" asked Chad.

"It doesn't," said Bianca.

"Just wait and see," Ben told them.

Ben poured the contents of three jars into the washing machine part.
The jars contained melted chocolate, melted butter and cream.

Oh No!

"When I pull this cord,"
Ben told the others,
"the washing machine part
will start shaking,
and will mix all the ingredients
together.
Then, the mixture will ooze down
the hose into this container.
Then, I'll have a container
of fresh, yummy ice-cream!"

Just then, there was a knock on the door.
Chad went to open the door while Ben pulled the cord.
In walked Chad's mum, dad and neighbour.

Instead of shaking around and around, the washing machine part flew into the air, turned upside down and dropped all the ingredients onto Ben's head.

"Is that your mum's washing machine part?" shouted Chad's mum.

"Is that your dad's starter cord from his lawn mower?" shouted Chad's dad.

"There's the missing piece of my garden hose!" shouted Frank, the neighbour.

"Oh no ..." Ben said.
"I think I'm in trouble."